MW01157150

SOLOS

for the

CLARINET
PLAYER

With Piano Accompaniment

Selected and Edited by

ARTHUR H. CHRISTMANN

ED. 2523

G. SCHIRMER, Inc.

DISTRIBUTED BY

HAL•LEONARD®
CORPORATION

7777 W. BLUEMOUND RD. P.O. BOX 13819 MILWAUKEE, WI 53213

Note

The present collection of clarinet pieces provides a repertory of solo material of medium difficulty. It includes a large number of pieces written originally for the instrument. Since the clarinet made its appearance late in music history, the Baroque heritage, which provides so much solo music for violin, flute, oboe, cello, etc., does not in the case of the clarinet. It is a little known fact that Vivaldi used clarinets in three of his *concerti grossi,* and there is some evidence that Handel wrote for the instrument in one instance. For all practical purposes any Baroque repertory played on the clarinet must be borrowed from that of other instruments. This is precisely what the present collection does.

Two criteria were used in the selection of the Baroque music: first, selections were chosen which the compiler uses in his own teaching and knows are ideally suited to the clarinet; second, it includes at least one composition of Bach, Handel and Vivaldi.

The original works presented begin with the Classic period and extend to the fairly recent. Many of them are the easier movements of major works for the instrument. A number of them are slow movements, for it is by interpreting slow music that the student learns phrasing and the experienced performer demonstrates deep insight. Clarinetists will be especially delighted with the slow movement from Carl Baermann's *Concerto Militaire,* a work which has long been out of print. Baermann is also represented by two etudes from the Second Division of his celebrated Clarinet Method. The *Valse triste* of Glière has a distinctly Chopinesque flavor. The Wagner composition is originally for clarinet and string quintet or string orchestra.

Editorial care has been taken to keep the expression marks in the style of the historical periods. In the Baroque transcriptions editing has been done on broad lines and marks of expression put in according to the principles of terraced, sectional dynamics. Thus the individual inflection of phrases is left to the interpretation of the performer and the suggestion of his teacher.

A.H.C.

CONTENTS

Index by Composers

1. Gavotte

Jean Baptiste Lully (1632–1687)
Arr. by A.H.C.

45472 cx

2. Allegro

from: Concerto for Oboe and Strings

Tommaso Albinoni, Op. 7, No. 6
(1671 - 1750)
Arr. by A. H. C.

3. First Movement

from: Flute Concerto in D, "*The Goldfinch*"

Antonio Vivaldi, Op. 10, No. 3
(c. 1678-1741)
Piano reduction by A. H. C.

4. Allegro

from: Flute Sonata in E

Johann Sebastian Bach (1685–1750)
Arr. by A.H.C.

5. Adagio and Allegro

from: Flute Sonata No. 3 in G

George Frideric Handel (1685-1759)
Arr. by A.H.C.

6. Sonata in G Major

(from the original for Cello)

I

Benedetto Marcello (1686 - 1739)
Arr. by A.H.C.

Andante

II

Allegro

III

IV

Allegro

7. Gavotte and Minuet

John Stanley (1713 - 1786)
Arr. by A.H.C.

Moderato e molto grazioso

8. Romance

from: Clarinet Concerto No. 3

Karl Stamitz (1745 - 1801)

9. Tambourin

Franz Joseph Gossec (1734 ~ 1829)
Arr. by A.H.C.

10. Larghetto

from: Quintet for Clarinet and Strings, K. 581

W. A. Mozart (1756 - 1791)
Piano reduction and arr. by A. H. C.

Larghetto

11. Adagio

from: Clarinet Concerto, K. 622

Wolfgang Amadeus Mozart
Revision and piano reduction
by Eric Simon

1) Suggested cadenza

12. Adagio

from: Concerto I

Ludwig Spohr (1784 - 1859), Op.26

13. Second Movement

from: Concerto No. 1 in F Minor

Carl Maria von Weber, Op. 73
(1786-1826)
Edited by Carl Baermann

14. Adagio

(Etude No. 24)

Carl Baermann, Op. 63
(1811 - 1885)

15. Fantasy Piece No. 1

Robert Schumann, Op. 73
(1810 - 1856)

16. Etude in B♭ Minor

(No. 47)

Carl Baermann, Op. 63

17. Second Movement

from: Concerto Militaire

Carl Baermann, Op. 6

18. Adagio for Clarinet

Richard Wagner (1813-1883)
Piano reduction by A. H. C.

19. Valse triste

Reinhold Glière, Op. 35, No. 7
(1875-1956)

20. Two Pieces
a. At the Brook

Mikhail Starokadomsky, Op. 22
(1901–1954)

Allegro giocoso

b. Intermezzo